Hey, God, I'm A Woman

Can You Use Me?!

by

Eva Gonzales

Hey, God, I'm a Woman; Can You Use Me?!

Sources consulted for this work include the following: *Ten Lies the Church Tells Women* by J. Lee Grady (Lake Mary, FL, Charisma House: 2000), *Male and Female Created He Them* by Bradford Scott (Wild Branch Ministry Tape Series: 1983), *Great Women in the Struggle* by Toyomi Igus, Veronica Freeman Ellis, Diane Patrick and Valarie Wilson (East Orange, NJ, Just Us Books, Inc.: 1991), *Keyword Study Bible* edited by Spiros Zodhiates (Chattanooga, TN, AMG Publishers:1991).

All biblical quotations are from the Authorized King James Version of the Bible.

McDougal Publishing is a ministry of The McDougal Foundation, Inc., a Maryland nonprofit corporation dedicated to spreading the Gospel of the Lord Jesus Christ to as many people as possible in the shortest time possible.

Published by:

McDougal Publishing
P.O. Box 3595
Hagerstown, MD 21742-3595

ISBN 13: 978-1-58158-117-1

Printed in the United States of America
For worldwide distribution

Dedication

This book is first dedicated to my heavenly Father, who has made this possible and would not let me give up. To the Godhead: You are the Vine, and I want so much to show off Your fruit on my branches.

To Dennis Gonzales, my husband and best friend: Thank you, Honey, for not being afraid to let me carry out the call of God on my life. You are my greatest inspiration and the wind beneath my wings.

To my darling daughter Trinity, who encouraged me to complete this project, allowing me time away: I know it was not easy.

To my son Joshua: You have made me glad. Mommy loves you.

Acknowledgments

A special thanks to the God-given staff at Fruit of the Spirit Ministries. Your support has made this possible in every way. I will always be grateful to you.

To Bill Yount: Our meeting was a divine appointment in so many ways.

I gratefully acknowledge my sisters, Irene Germaine, Hazel Wilson and LeAine Dehmer, who always told me the truth, whether I wanted to hear it or not. Your advice is priceless to me. Thank you for your love and input.

To Barbara Shaw: Nothing is lost. Thank you. The best is yet to come.

Contents

Let your women keep silence in the churches: for it is not permitted unto them to speak; but they are commanded to be under obedience, as also saith the law.

1 Corinthians 14:34

But I suffer not a woman to teach nor usurp authority over the man but to be in silence. For Adam was first formed then Eve.

1 Timothy 2:12-13

For as many of you as have been baptized into Christ have put on Christ. There is neither Jew nor Greek, there is neither bond nor free, there is neither male nor female: for ye are all one in Christ Jesus. And if ye be Christ's, then are ye Abraham's seed, and heirs according to the promise.

Galatians 3:27-29

Introduction

This book has been a long time in coming. It could have contained many more pages, but I knew in my spirit that God was impressing upon me to reduce it to a concise study, so that anyone desiring to be informed regarding this subject can read it in one or two sittings.

Whether or not God can use a woman in public ministry has long been a very controversial subject. I wrote this book, not to be right regarding this matter, but in search of truth.

I pray that this little book will be read by many and prove thought-provoking to them. If there is any doubt about the research I present here, please study the subject for yourself. Do it prayerfully and with an open heart. In our modern world, we must properly educate ourselves, according to the truth of God's Word, and eliminate any unnecessary, outdated cultural traditions, thus giving all glory to God alone.

Let's get started.

Pastor Eva Gonzales
Santa Fe, New Mexico

CHAPTER 1

THE LIMITATIONS OF FOLLOWING TRADITION AND NOT TRUTH

Thus have ye made the commandment of God of none effect by your tradition. Matthew 15:6

I was told a story about a young girl who got married and was cooking a ham for the holidays. Her husband passed by the kitchen and saw her cutting the end off of the ham, and he asked her, "Why do you cut the end off like that?" It was his favorite part of the meat.

She said, "I don't know. Momma always did it."

His question left a lingering doubt in her mind. So as soon as she had the opportunity, she called her mother and asked her: "Why do we always cut the end off a ham before baking it?"

Her mother's reply, very much like her own, was simply, "I don't know. My mother always did it."

Next the young woman called her Granny. "Granny," she said, "why do we cut the end off a ham before we cook it?"

Granny's answer was a surprising one and should open our eyes to the limitations of many of our long-held traditions. "Baby, we couldn't afford a larger pan," she said laughingly, "and so, cutting off the end of the ham was the only way I could get it to fit the pan we had."

Isn't that an amazing story? Somehow, that simple act, brought about because of a physical limitation, had become a tradition in the family, and was continued long after it was necessary. In two generations, no one knew exactly why this unexplained tradition continued by future generations. It just seemed like the proper thing to do.

My prayer is that, with all the tools God has blessed us with for research into His will and His Word in this twenty-first century, we will no longer be satisfied to allow our outdated cultures and traditions (handed-down beliefs) to limit the Word of God and make the Word of God *"of none effect."*

If we believe something, we need a good reason for believing it, and the fact that others believed it before us is not a good enough reason. For those of us who love God and love His Word, let's be faithful to study to show ourselves approved unto Him, as the Scriptures so aptly admonish us:

> *Study to show yourself approved unto God, a workman that needeth not to be ashamed, rightly dividing the word of truth.* 2 Timothy 2:15

No matter what you believe regarding this subject of women in ministry, be willing to take another look. Most people have never studied this subject for themselves, and, consequently, they limit themselves by conforming to tradition only repeating what they've heard others say. I always say to myself, "If there's a *right* way to divide the Word of truth, then there must also be a *wrong* way to divide it." This is the reason each of us must study and research the truth for ourselves.

In order to see the Body of Christ come into maturity in these days, each and every one of us needs to be in his or her proper place. This includes men, women, boys and girls. Anyone who is out of place will only lend strength to the enemy. Therefore, in the days to come, we must live by the teaching of God's Word to the Ephesians:

> *And He gave some apostles; and some prophets; and some evangelists; and some pastors; and teachers. For the perfecting [maturing] of the saints, for the work of the ministry, for the edifying of the body of Christ. Till we all come in the unity of the faith, and of the knowledge of the Son of God unto a perfect man, unto the measure of the stature of the fullness of Christ.*
>
> *That we henceforth be no more children tossed to and fro, and carried about with every wind of doc-*

trine, by the sleight of men, and cunning craftiness, whereby they lie in wait to deceive; but speaking the truth in love, may grow up into him in all things, which is the head, even Christ: from whom the whole body fitly joined together and compacted by that which every joint supplieth, according to the effectual working in the measure of every part, make increase of the body unto the edifying of itself in love.

Ephesians 4:11-16

There are several important phrases here that we need to examine more fully and be sure to heed:

That we henceforth be no more children tossed to and fro, and carried about with every wind of doctrine, by the sleight of men, and cunning craftiness, whereby they lie in wait to deceive.

Hindering women from public ministry because of our miseducation and ancient traditions is childish and destructive. It not only limits the women who are suppressed; it also limits the whole Body of Christ.

Paul dealt with mind set back in New Testament days:

... grow up into him in all things, which is the head,

even Christ: from whom the whole body fitly joined together and compacted by that which every joint supplieth, according to the effectual working in the measure of every part,

Did he say *THE WHOLE BODY*? Then he must have meant *THE WHOLE BODY*.

Did he say *EVERY JOINT*? Then he must have meant *EVERY JOINT*.

Did he say *EVERY PART?* Then he must have meant *EVERY PART*.

So why are we holding back a major portion of believers with our worn-out, outdated and short-sighted traditions? When any doctrine, no matter how long it has been held or how widely accepted it is, contradicts other parts of God's Word, there's something wrong with it. And the doctrine that prevents women from occupying their God-given place in the Body of Christ is just such a doctrine.

If there's one thing I've learned about truth (which the Word of God exemplifies), it's that it will stand forever. Tradition has to give way.

Hey, God, I'm a Woman; Can You Use Me?!

Chapter 2

Where Did All the Confusion Come From?

> *Let your women keep silence in the churches: for it is not permitted unto them to speak; but they are commanded to be under obedience, as also saith the law.* 1 Corinthians 14:34

We cannot deny that the apostle Paul wrote these words in his first letter to the Corinthian believers, and this verse is the source of much of the controversy over the subject of women in ministry today. Why did he make such a statement?

For one thing, it says, *"Keep silence."* Far too many ministers take that phrase literally without ever considering why Paul would make such a statement. And yet ministers who try to enforce the rule of women keeping silence in the church often don't completely believe it themselves. *Silence* in the English language has only one definition; it means "silence," don't make a sound. So that alone raises a few serious questions in my mind.

Why, if women are to *"keep silence"* in the church, are they permitted to sing, to make important announcements, to teach Sunday school and to lead women's ministries? When this happens, are the men in charge just compromising to satisfy a need in the church? Or was it always God's intention for men and women to work together for His glory? These are the questions I want to answer for my generation.

This phrase "keep silence" was also used to admonish a man who spoke in an unknown tongue without an interpreter. If we could keep these verses in context, it would be clearly understood that Paul was establishing order versus confusion (see Verse 40).

Also, the word *women* in verse 34 should not be translated *women* in the generic sense, but as *wives*.

I want to thank God for placing these matters in my care. With the love I have for the Lord, it is not my desire to disobey Him. If it was God's will for a woman to keep silent, then you can believe that silent is what I would want to be. Consequently, I've done a lot of research on the subject and am convinced that keeping women locked out of public ministry is *not* God's will and never has been. And if you are a woman and have been denied the right to fulfill your calling in God, I believe that you, too, will walk in revelation and strength by the time you're done reading this book.

Let's get right to the point, and, by using bite-sized pieces that we can easily digest, let's attempt to educate ourselves in the truth of this matter. I pray that all legalism and selfish ambition will leave the leadership of God's Church today. There are no big I's and little you's in His Kingdom. Rather, the Kingdom of God is *"righteousness, ... peace, and joy in the Holy Ghost":*

> *For the kingdom of God is not meat and drink; but righteousness, and peace, and joy in the Holy Ghost.*
>
> Romans 14:17

That's the Kingdom way.

Today, as never before, we need each other functioning in our God-given purpose so that we can defeat a mutual enemy. Satan is a mastermind of deception. Anything that he can do to delay Christ's coming and bring confusion among the believers, he will not hesitate to do it.

It's very sad to see that there are many women out there with a true call of God upon their lives, but they cannot step out because they've been told by some church leader who was miseducated that God can't use women in the five-fold ministry of apostles, prophets, evangelists, pastors and teachers.

With all the controversy surrounding this subject some times I wonder to myself did God forget that I was a woman when He appeared to me? What about the women He used in the Bible who carried out specific assignments? There was Deborah, Priscilla, Anna, Phebe and Esther, and we could go on and on.

Should He have sought the approval of someone here on Earth before He inspired these many women?

These are all things we all need to consider. If what you believe is truth, it will survive any amount of scrutiny from any source and go on standing forever.

Jesus said, regarding His words:

> *Heaven and earth shall pass away, but my words shall not pass away.* Matthew 24:35

Therefore, we should govern our daily lives by that which is true. Again, Jesus said (this time to the Father):

> *Sanctify them through thy truth: thy word is truth.* John 17:17

Jesus also said that we would be known by the love we have for each other, not by the level of competition we have with one another.

I know firsthand what can result when God's people are miseducated because they have been misinformed and are being held back by someone else's lack of information. After all, I'm not only a woman; I'm also of Black decent, and, furthermore, I was raised in the South. I still remember when there were segregated restrooms and water fountains because our people were not considered to be totally human. It was a very common misconception that Blacks were far inferior to Caucasians. Even some of *us* became convinced that we had little or nothing to contribute to society, when all along ours were the backs upon which this nation was built. We were forced to work, much like the Hebrews in captivity in Egypt. However, God had a plan for our people. We were important to the development of America and the world.

It was an important point in American history when we began to stand up for what we believed. Many gave their lives for our freedom, and gradually, things got better for us. They're still not what they should be, but they're also not what they used to be.

When this severe racial discrimination was being carried out against us, we blacks, as a people, knew in our hearts that we were not mere animals, as some claimed we were. For a long while, the myth continued to swirl about that we actually had tails like monkeys and just hid them. What an insult to the Creator's intelligence!

It's not hard to see why all of this happened. The enemy wanted to keep us in slavery, but God had other plans, and it was His truth that eventually set us free. That same knowing that was inside of every Black person is inside of every woman in the Body of Christ today who has been genuinely called by God into ministry.

I know how fear can grip when one stands for truth. Taking a stand means getting hit, and hits are painful. I have battled hell to write this book. But it had to be done.

Hey, God, I'm a Woman; Can You Use Me?!

Chapter 3

Why the Devil Hates Woman

And I will put enmity between you and the woman, and between your seed and her seed; it shall bruise your head and you shall bruise his heel.

Genesis 3:15

Let's take a look at the first woman and her dealings with the serpent, for an understanding of why the father of lies (Satan) hates women so much. God said He would put *"enmity"* between the woman and the serpent, and sure enough, until now most women don't like snakes, and Satan surely hates us. Not only did the woman introduce a serious problem, but God also used her to bring a serious solution.

We first see the snake in verse one of this chapter, and there the Bible says *"the serpent was more subtle than any beast of the field"* (Genesis 3:1). He was *"subtle,"* or cunning. He approached the woman with evil intent, and he accused God from the very start.

His question to the woman was this: *"Yea, hath God said?"* (Genesis 3:1). He was questioning God's authority and His integrity, and in the process, he was sowing doubt in the mind of the woman against her God.

What was the woman's intent? I believe the woman's original intent was to correct or explain to the serpent that he had been misinformed. She told him that God had given her and Adam permission to eat of the fruit of the trees of the garden, and she then pointed out God's specific instruction to them regarding *"the tree in the midst of the garden"* (Genesis 3:3). They were not to eat of it (not even, Eve added, to touch it). If they did, they would die.

It was then that the serpent pulled out his bag of tricks full of lies and persuasion, and he proceeded to persuade the woman that God's instructions to them had been flawed. His words were limiting, and therefore they were not the best for her and her husband.

Next, the enemy began to deal with her fleshly senses. He used her eye gate, and verse 6 declares: *"and when the woman SAW."* This is an all-too-common tactic of Satan. He always appeals to our five senses. The Bible names *"the lust of the flesh, the lust of the eyes, and the pride of life"* as the traps set for the whole human race (1 John 2:16). Beware!

For a moment, the woman took her eyes off of all the other trees of the garden and focused on what the enemy was saying, and the result was that she became selfish through what she heard coming from his mouth. This is the power of persuasion. Protect yourself from what you hear when it exalts itself above God's Word.

Because of listening to the enemy, she turned her back on the trust that she'd had in Almighty God.

Now convinced that God did not have her best interests at heart, she began to doubt Him.

The power of persuasion can be deadly. We must know who we're listening to and then take it back to God in prayer. In the very same way, Satan has persuaded many in the Body of Christ that women are not to be used by God in public ministry. Just as he conned Eve into disbelieving God's clear instructions to her, he is crippling generations and keeping them from the truth of God's Word.

I have read and researched great intellectuals who have written on this subject and do not take into consideration the mindset of the first century regarding the female gender. These may be sincere in their writing, but I believe they are sincerely incorrect or misinformed and what they say brings about great division in the Body of Christ.

Like Eve, when we hear Satan's lies, we often fail to go back to God and reaffirm what He has said before drawing our final conclusion. We would rather remain comfortable in our own conclusions and not be challenged in our thinking regarding handed-down beliefs. It's always easier just to believe what we've been taught than to seek out the truth. Besides, prayer and seeking God is work.

So, we go on believing that what we've been taught is the Gospel, without really studying the matter for ourselves. Most people don't bother to read God's Word, so how could they possibly know the truth?

I'm convinced that Jesus will always answer a sincere heart that is open to truth. Nicodemus asked Him, *"How can a man be born when he is old?"* (John 3:4), and he got his answer.

Zacchaeus had a sincere heart to see Jesus because he knew there were something special about this Man. When Jesus passed by the sycamore tree, therefore, He called Zacchaeus and gave him an experience he would never forget.

These men were sincere in their hearts, and they got answers. On the other hand, when the leading religious sects of Jesus' day (the Pharisees, Sadducees and scribes) tried to trick Him through their questions, He called them just what they were—*"hypocrites"* (Matthew 15:7). On one occasion, He even told them: *"Ye are of your father the devil"* (John 8:44). I've said all of that to say this: It is not enough to take someone's word regarding the truth. We must be like the Bereans. They searched the Scriptures to find the truth:

> *These were more noble than those in Thessalonica, in that they received the word with all readiness of mind, and searched the scriptures daily, whether those things were so.* Acts 17:11

Once more I repeat: Jesus will always answer a sincere heart with truth. Have you ever been wrong about something that you sincerely believed?

Now, let's get back to Eden and the enmity that developed between the woman and the serpent.

This word *enmity*, in Hebrew, means "ill will, mutual hatred." Satan doesn't like women in the first place, so do you think he will allow a woman to function for God without giving her a fight? It was, indeed, the woman who first brought chaos into the world, but now God would use her to bring the solution to the problem. It was Eve's offspring who would bring forth the Son of God, so if I were Satan, I would do just what he is doing, try to convince everyone that women have no place in God's work. Could Satan know something about women that mankind has not stopped to figure out yet? Does Satan understand reproduction better than people do, that he would approach Eve and not Adam?

It seems to me that the Church is not willing to consider the subtleties of the enemy, the unseen spiritual divisiveness waging warfare against us all. The enemy knows the importance of the woman's contribution to humanity and our spirituality. I could speak on homosexuality and lesbianism here, but that's for another book. That's why, when it comes to cults and doctrines of demons, he normally presents a woman to be worshipped.

In the Catholic Church, he has presented us the Queen of Heaven. The Church has actually made Mary equal to Christ. I have nothing against the Catholic Church. I grew up Catholic and attended Catholic school. I even thought I wanted to be a nun, and I was taught the New Testament in Catholic school. I love my Catholic brethren. But Mary worship is not pleasing to God. Only He is to be worshiped:

> *Hear, O Israel: The* Lord *our God is one* Lord.
>
> Deuteronomy 6:4

In Paul's day, the enemy presented to the Ephesians the great goddess Diana, and the worship of her brought much gain to the local craftsmen (see Acts 19:24). Generation after generation has worshiped female deities, but when it comes to Christianity, the true faith, Satan has convinced us that women are not even important enough to be heard.

Can't you see the cunning behind this tactic? Having people believe his lie lightens the load against Satan. But God cannot lie. If He says something, then you can "take it to the bank."

God promised the serpent that ***the seed of the woman*** would bruise his head. Think about that for a moment. Women don't have seed; only men do. In fulfillment, God brought forth a man-child from a woman without the benefit of seed from a man.

And why not? In the beginning, God took a grown man, and out of him, He produced a grown woman. So why couldn't God take a woman and out of her produce a manchild, without the help of another man?

God is never without a plan. Everything that He created was good. The first time we hear Him say that something was *"not good"* was when He said:

*It is not good for man to be alone.*Genesis 2:18

After God had made everything, including Adam, He crowned creation with the gift of a woman, like icing on a cake. This gift changed Adam's entire perspective. Now he was able to reproduce himself, and he had a suitable companion.

Until that moment, Adam had been limited. He had watched the animals reproduce after their kind, and he saw vegetation reproduce after its kind, and yet he could not reproduce like everything else in nature. He was not compatible with any of the other created life forms around him. God solved Adam's dilemma, and his solution was woman.

The enemy, I believe, was aware of the changes for good that had come to Adam, when he saw the man and the woman interacting. He knew then that God had given the man something very special. This, to me, explains why he approached the woman and not the man.

Adam was the final authority in the family, so why did the serpent not go straight to him? What did he observe in the relationship between the man and the woman that caused him to have a conversation with the woman rather than with the man directly? I believe he observed her ability to reproduce.

Adam was no longer alone, he could now reproduce himself, and he had a higher level of joy and comfort. This was due to the gift of the woman in his life. Because of this, I believe Satan understood that the gift of reproduction brings forth birthing, and he wanted to establish his plan against God by birthing his purpose through the woman. God, in turn, used the woman to reinforce His purpose for the human race and to bring restoration. The woman, in short, is always the birther. That may not be considered a word in the English language, but it is in my revelation from God.

Satan always perverts what's good. His intentions are to defile and twist all that which is holy, but God has a handle on everything, even when we can't figure it out.

In the end, Genesis 3:15 (the first prophecy given to mankind) was fulfilled in what transpired in Luke 1:26-38. This is a prophetic passage that came from the heart and mouth of God, and was fulfilled when Jesus was conceived in the womb of a young virgin named Mary.

Luke tells the story like this:

> *And in the sixth month the angel Gabriel was sent from God unto a city of Galilee named Nazareth. To a virgin espoused to a man whose name was Joseph of the house of David; and the virgin's name was Mary. And the angel came in unto her, and said, Hail thou that art highly favoured, the Lord is with you; blessed art you among women.*
>
> *And when she saw him, she was troubled at his saying, and cast in her mind what manner of salu-*

tation this should be. And the angel said unto her. Fear not, Mary: for thou hast found favour with God. And behold, thou shall conceive in your womb, and bring forth a son, and shall call his name JESUS. He shall be great, and shall be called the Son of the Highest: and the Lord God shall give unto him the throne of his father David. And he shall reign over the house of Jacob forever; and of his kingdom there shall be no end.

Then said Mary unto the angel, How shall this be, seeing I know not a man?

And the angel answered and said unto her, The Holy Ghost shall come upon you, and the power of the Highest shall overshadow you: therefore also that holy thing which shall be born of you shall be called the Son of God. And, behold, your cousin Elisabeth, she hath also conceived a son in her old age: and this is the sixth month with her, who was called barren. For with God nothing shall be impossible.

And Mary said, Behold the handmaid of the Lord; be it unto me according to thy word. And the angel departed from her. Luke 1:26-38

There are several things I want us to look at more closely in this passage. First, it's important that Mary *"was a virgin."* Did not the prophets, after Genesis 3:15, continue to declare what God had decreed? For instance, Isaiah said:

> *Therefore the Lord himself shall give you a sign; Behold, a virgin shall conceive, and bear a son, and shall call his name Immanuel.* Isaiah 7:14

> *For unto us a child is born, unto us a son is given: and the government shall be upon his shoulder; and his name shall be called Wonderful, Counselor, The Mighty God, The everlasting Father, The Prince of Peace.* Isaiah 9:6

The second thing I want us to notice in this passage is that this Child, born of God, was connected to King David of old. We will look more at that later.

We must also notice the fact that not even Mary's fiancee believed her. He was ready to put her away privately, or secretly, but then God came to him in a dream and told him not to do it (see Matthew 1:19). I've learned that God can use anyone who is willing to yield to Him. People may not believe you, but if you'll be diligent to obey God at all costs, He will work for you.

When Mary said, *"Be it unto me,"* she was fulfilling God's promise that the seed of the woman would bruise the head of the serpent. The seed of the woman came from God, by the Holy Spirit, when He *"overshadowed"* Mary. Nothing sexual had to happen because, *"with God, all things are possible"* (Matthew 19:26).

God could have made another man from the dust of the ground and put His Spirit into him, but His principle is that everything that He made has its seed in itself. Some ask: What came first, the chicken or the egg? For me, that's an easy question to answer. The chicken came first, because the principle of God says that the seed would be in the thing so that it could reproduce (see Genesis 1). Also, this child Jesus, fully God and fully man, had to be able to relate to humanity in order to redeem men.

Now back to David: God promised David that his heir would always be on the throne of Israel:

> *And as since the time I commanded judges to be over my people Israel, and have caused thee to rest from all thine enemies.*
> *Also the Lord tell you that he will make you a house. And when your days be fulfilled, and you shall sleep with your fathers, I will set up your seed after you, which shall proceed out of your bowels, and I will establish his kingdom. He shall build a house for my name, and I will establish the throne of his kingdom forever.* 2 Samuel 7:11-13

This referred initially to Solomon, but ultimately the reference was to Jesus Christ, the Son of David, who reigns at God's right hand (see Psalm 2:7 and Acts 13:33).

So, it was all fulfilled in Jesus, born of a woman. *Hey, God, I'm a Woman; Can You Use Me?!*

Chapter 4

God's Call Is Our Strongest Argument

> *For as many of you as have been baptized into Christ have put on Christ. There is neither Jew nor Greek, there is neither bond nor free, there is neither male nor female: for ye are all one in Christ Jesus. And if ye be Christ's, then are ye Abraham's seed, and heirs according to the promise.*
>
> Galatians 3:27-29

Neither male nor female.

Ye are all one in Christ Jesus—men and women alike.

Then are ye Abraham's seed, and heirs—regardless of gender.

God proved this by calling us, and to my way of thinking, His call is our strongest argument. If God has called us, then who dares to oppose us? I don't ask this to be disrespectful to men, but to be obedient to the One who called me:

> *Then Peter and the other apostles answered and said, We ought to obey God rather than men.* Acts 5:29

To any person, male or female, who desires to be in ministry but is not sure they've been extended an invitation from God, I would say in the strongest terms, Please, go do something else. The ministry is not a cake walk; it's serious business. But if God has indeed called you, how can you not respond—regardless of what others might choose to think?

After 9/11 took place and we were able to see into the Islamic nations, what we saw shocked us. But when I saw how women were being treated in those nations, I could not help but think that this was exactly what women looked like in the Spirit in our American churches. A few escape the confinement, but if we would all apply God's Word to our daily lives, we would be much further down the road to fulfillment of God's plan for us than we are today.

One thing I know; I'm a survivor because God has built it into me. Some call it rebellion, a Jezebel spirit and only God knows what else (again, another book to come). In my heart, I know that what I do is motivated by my love for God and my desire not to fail Him in any way. Sitting down and doing nothing would be the easiest thing in the world, but would it be the right thing to do? No way!

God called women throughout the Bible. If Paul was against women speaking in church and meant First Timothy 2:12 literally (according to our current understanding of the English language), *"But I suffer not a woman to teach, nor to usurp authority over the man, but to be in silence,"* why then would he have allowed Phebe, a woman, to deliver his letter to the Church at Rome (see Romans 16:1)? Were there men in that church? In verse 3 he honored Priscilla as well as Aquila.

I don't want to sound defensive, but we need to do our homework. I have to ask you, dear reader: Have you studied this matter out for yourself? Or are you also guilty of simply repeating what you've heard others say?

Here's a question to consider: What gender is the biblical term *"Zion"*? What gender is the Bride of Christ? And do you consider yourself to be part of either of these blessed groups? Of course you do. So, who said that God can't use the female gender?

It was a woman who carried the Word of God in her womb before man ever believed it was possible. Joseph, her fiancee, was ready to put Mary away privately, and he would have done it, if God had not intervened supernaturally. Maybe God will have to do that same thing again today, intervening supernaturally in some way, to prove to us that He can still use women. He can even use a donkey if He wants to.

Jesus commissioned a woman to go tell His disciples that He was risen, when He knew very well that the word of a woman carried no weight with Jewish men of that day. This shows me that our Lord intended for things to change, and that's more true today than ever before. It's time to change, beloved! For those who have ears to hear, hear what the Spirit is saying to the churches.

Jewish men of that time were known to pray, "God, thank You for not making me a woman." But hatred and disrespect for women comes from the spirit of the enemy, never from God. Times change, traditions change and men change, but God never does. I like what Gamaliel said to the religious leaders of his day:

> *Then stood there up one in the council, a Pharisee, named Gamaliel, a doctor of the law, had in reputation among all the people, and commanded to put the apostles forth a little space; and said unto them, Ye men of Israel, take heed to yourselves what ye intend to do as touching these men. And now I say unto you, Refrain from these men, and let them alone: for if this counsel or this work be of men, it will come to nought: but if it be of God, ye cannot overthrow it; lest haply ye be found even to fight against God.*
>
> Acts 5:34-35 and 38-39

This is a serious issue. If we find ourselves fighting God, we're all in trouble.

So should a woman preach the Gospel? Can a

woman pastor a church? These are not insignificant issues.

Personally, I've been talked about, laughed at, lied on, told I was out of order—all because I decided I had to obey God. He never goes against His Word, so if He can use a woman, the answer has to be found somewhere in His Word.

I believe the reason God allowed T.D. Jakes' powerful message, *Woman, Thou Art Loosed,* to go far and wide is that it was birthed in the Father's own heart. I want to repeat his use of this wonderful scripture: *"Woman, thou art loosed"* (Luke 13:12). Woman was loosed when the angel appeared to Mary, and she replied, *"Be it unto me according to thy word"* (Luke 1:38). Woman was loosed when Jesus healed the woman who had been bowed over for eighteen long years (see Luke 13:11-13). Woman was loosed when He delivered the woman at the well (see John 4:5-26). Woman was loosed when He sent her to go tell even His disciples that He had risen (see Matthew 28:7). If that wasn't preaching the Gospel, then I don't know what is. God's call upon us is our strongest argument. He never makes mistakes.

Under the circumstances, why was this woman not afraid to speak to the disciples? When God burns truth into your heart and then commands you to tell it, you simply can't keep quiet. Ask the woman at the well; ask the prophet Jeremiah about it:

> *Then I said, I will not make mention of him, nor speak any more in his name. But his word was in mine heart as a burning fire shut up in my bones, and I was weary with forbearing, and I could not stay.*
> *For I heard the defaming of many, fear on every side. Report, say they, and we will report it. All my familiars watched for my halting, saying, Peradventure he will be enticed, and we shall prevail against him, and we shall take our revenge on him.*
> *But the Lord is with me as a mighty terrible one: therefore my persecutors shall stumble, and they shall not prevail: they shall be greatly ashamed; for they shall not prosper: their everlasting confusion shall never be forgotten.* Jeremiah 20:9-11

When God first called me into the ministry I, too, had a question for Him. Why was there no woman called to be part of the twelve? He answered me this way: "I came to fulfill the Law. Now that the Law has been fulfilled, a new covenant I give unto you." That new covenant is better known to most of us as the New Testament, and no sooner had this new period begun than God chose a woman to go tell everyone about it—even the eleven remaining disciples (all men). That sounds to me like a powerful argument for change.

Hey, God, I'm a Woman; Can You Use Me?!

Chapter 5

What Was the Creator's Original Intent?

And God blessed them, and God said unto them, Be fruitful, and multiply, and replenish the earth, and subdue it: and have dominion over the fish of the sea, and over the fowl of the air, and over every living thing that moveth upon the earth. Genesis 1:28

God didn't just bless one of them; He blessed both of *them*. He didn't just pronounce fruitfulness over one of them; He pronounced it over both of *them*. He didn't just commission one of them; He commissioned both of *them*. He commissioned them at the very same moment, and He commissioned them to do the very same work. Functioning separately they establish a position; functioning as God intended they walk in dominion.

Just as women are an integral and important part of every marriage and of every family, women are also an integral and important part of the Body of Christ (someday soon to be His Bride). As such, we are created to carry out the will of God wherever we are needed—just as men are. Men and women were not created to work apart from each other. We were designed by God to work together. *God blessed THEM.*

When God created man, He did it with purpose, and when He created woman, He also had a purpose in doing it. His creation of man (of whom woman is an integral part) is recounted again in the very next chapter of Genesis, this time in a little more detail:

> *And the LORD God formed man of the dust of the ground, and breathed into his nostrils the breath of life; and man became a living soul.*
>
> Genesis 2:7

> *And the LORD God said, It is not good that the man should be alone; I will make him an help meet for him. And out of the ground the LORD God formed every beast of the field, and every fowl of the air; and brought them unto Adam to see what he would call them: and whatsoever Adam called every living creature, that was the name thereof. And Adam gave names to all cattle, and to the fowl of the air, and to every beast of the field; but for Adam there was not found an help meet for him.*
>
> *And the LORD God caused a deep sleep to fall upon Adam, and he slept: and he took one of his ribs,*

and closed up the flesh instead thereof; and the rib, which the L*ORD God had taken from man, made he a woman, and brought her unto the man. And Adam said, This is now bone of my bones, and flesh of my flesh: she shall be called Woman, because she was taken out of Man. Therefore shall a man leave his father and his mother, and shall cleave unto his wife: and they shall be one flesh.*

Genesis 2:18-24

Yes, we must recognize that man was created first, we must also recognize that he was incomplete, and God was not satisfied that man was alone. God then made a woman from the man and, with that, declared His work to be finished. Man was incomplete without woman, so woman completes man, and the two were made for each other. The two became one.

Woman was given to man as a helpmeet, not as his slave or his servant. There is nothing about the creation that can make us believe that God somehow made the female to be inferior to or less important than the male.

I remember the first time I saw an Asian woman walking behind her husband. The Asian women do this because they're not considered to be worthy to walk beside their husbands. There was something about that scene that just didn't look right, as if even nature knew better. To me, that kind of understanding should come naturally, if man would just keep his hands off of God's natural order of things.

Believe me, Jesus does not call His Bride to walk behind Him, so why should any natural man require it? Can you even imagine our Lord Jesus telling His Bride, "You must walk behind Me." Personally, I can't imagine it.

If, for some reason, God said such a thing, I would gladly obey, because none of us is worthy of walking with the God of Heaven. And yet, by His grace, He has permitted us to walk by His side.

Our Lord is never abusive, not even to vile sinners, so we should never fear to walk with Him. Jesus finds no reason to belittle His Bride; He is totally secure, and besides, He truly loves us. Therefore we should teach Ephesians 5:28 every bit as much as we teach Ephesians 5:22:

> *So ought men to love their wives as their own bodies. He that loveth his wife loveth himself.*
>
> Ephesians 5:28

> *Wives, submit yourselves unto your own husbands, as unto the Lord.* Ephesians 5:22

The two verses go together, and if we taught them in a balanced way, it would bring great joy to the Body of Christ.

Ephesians 2:6 shows us the position the Bride will assume with Her heavenly Bridegroom. We will not only walk together; we will sit together (see Ephesians 2:6).

Satan wants us to believe a lie, that a bride is inferior to her bridegroom. There is so much power in his suggestion that it has divided churches, households and relationships. It's time for all that to end. This was not the original intent of the Creator. He made man and woman to walk together and to work together.

Hey, God, I'm a Woman; Can You Use Me?!

Chapter 6

Respecting God's Order

Wives, submit yourselves unto your own husbands, as unto the Lord. Ephesians 5:22

God is a God of order, and He has established an order regarding the family and an order regarding the Church family. Every married woman should respect her husband and treat him like the king he is. The Scriptures are clear on this point.

For my part, God has blessed me with a very good husband, a man who encourages me to fulfill God's call on my life. I'm so thankful for such a man, and I love him so much that I'll do anything (in line with God's Word) to please him. That's the kind of marriage our Creator envisioned.

So women need to get their attitudes adjusted concerning the men in their lives. But there's another side to this issue. Man was called to love his wife as he loves himself. Men are initiators; women are responders. It was Adam's responsibility to cover and protect Eve. Because Adam did not take authority he placed Eve in a vulnerable position. Remember Eve was deceived; Adam was not. Let's look at that passage again:

> *So ought men to love their wives as their own bodies. He that loveth his wife loveth himself.*
>
> Ephesians 5:28

Wow! That's a powerful love. Such a love would not deny a woman her rightful place in the marriage, in the home, in the church or in the community.

The work of God is not limited to gender or age. When God sent a woman to tell the eleven disciples that He had risen, if she was not allowed to tell men anything, then God violated His own Word. And He would never do that. We have been miseducated.

Please don't misunderstand me. This book is not against men in any way. I love and highly respect this creature God Himself has created and placed on Earth. I'm believing for the day when we can all—men and women—walk together hand-in-hand, doing the work and the will of God according to His original intent.

In the natural, when a man and woman come into unity in marriage, children are born of that union. Fruitfulness and multiplication happens. Think of it! Satan must tremble with fear at the very thought of seeing "men and women" take their rightful place in the Kingdom of God, walking with true understanding of His purposes for us all.

It was this very theme of God's order that led to many of Paul's statements in his letters to Timothy.

Timothy was still a very young man, but even at that age, he had been given an important responsibility. He was pastor over a huge church in Ephesus. Therefore, in writing to his son in the faith, Paul was encouraging Timothy to be responsible, regardless of the heavy burdens he was facing. He warned Timothy to protect the church from the infiltration of myths and false doctrines. The pastor's responsibility is to combat false teaching with sound doctrine.

It's important to remember that Christianity was a very new religion at that time, and Paul was the man God chose to become a voice of maturity, a spiritual father, to many of the Gentile churches. There was, no doubt, because he had founded many of them himself and the people knew and trusted him. It was also because he had a special anointing for this work.

Regarding Timothy, the foundation of the church had to be laid in truth, for he had to be strong enough to then challenge every myth and wrong doctrine that would try to creep into the church in the days ahead.

There is another important element in this equation that we must understand. At the time Paul wrote his letter to Timothy, there existed a sect known as the Gnostics. Gnosticism was made up of many different beliefs, somewhat like the many New Age groups of our day. God's Word is the same for every individual, as we find it written to the Galatians:

I marvel that you are turning away so soon from Him who called you in the grace of Christ to a different gospel. Which is not another; but there are some who trouble you and want to pervert the gospel of Christ. But even if we or an angel from heaven, preach any other gospel to you than what we have preached to you, let him be accursed.

Galatians 1:6-8

It was to address the error of the Gnostics and others that Paul wrote as he did. It was all a matter of order:

But let all things be done decently and in order.

1 Corinthians 14:40

This is a principle that applies to all churches everywhere and in every age. Just as doing things in order doesn't hinder a man or disallow his call, there is no reason to believe that the correct order for the church should in any way hinder the special call of a woman. Order brings liberty, not bondage. It brings fulfillment, not repression.

Hey, God, I'm a Woman; Can You Use Me?!

Chapter 7

The High Price of Freedom

And the chief captain answered, With a great sum obtained I this freedom. And Paul said, But I was free born. Acts 22:28

Before moving on, I want to explore a little more of this matter concerning our freedom from a racial discrimination perspective, because there is such a strong corollary between what we suffered in this regard and what women currently suffer in the Church.

My ancestors paid a high price to be here. Enduring the extremely harsh treatment on the slave ships, gave them a toughening spirit of survival. We must admit that the wilderness was good for us, because it brought forth strengths we didn't realize we had.

I cannot forget the way my grandmother, Mrs. Flossie Lindsey, fought for our freedom. I was just three when, in 1963, she went to Washington, D.C. with other Civil Rights leaders to meet with our President and make him see that it was not right how the Black man and his family were being treated. Thank you, Momma. I hope you're proud of me. I learned from the best.

My grandmother fought so that I could have the right to an education and grow up and have the freedom of choice, like children of other races. It seemed that she and other committed Civil Rights leaders were making progress because they soon put some of us into an all-white school in Mississippi. I look back now and realize that, in a sense, they sacrificed us (their most prized possession) to prove to this nation that change had to come.

In 1966 I attended first grade in an all-white school. Only a few blacks from our neighborhood were allowed to attend. When recess came, I naturally sought out my friends on the playground. Noting this, my teacher kept me during the next recess. "You musn't play with those darker-skinned children," she told me. I was only six and very impressionable. I didn't understand what my light skin color had to do with my friends.

When those children next came to visit my home, I told them that I was no longer allowed to play with them. Overhearing this conversion, my mother asked me what was going on. I explained to her that Mrs. McDonald said for me not to play with those other children because they were "too dark." Mother went to see the teacher and to tell the other Civil Rights leaders about this. I feel that both Mother and my grandmother made great strides in helping to bring equality to my generation. They've been instrumental in my being able to read and have the freedom to write a book like this without being stoned to death or put in jail.

My mother and grandmother made me believe that all men are created equal. I was told that God loved us all the same. No one was better than another in His eyes. God never thought any less of us because of our skin color. After all, we all came from Him.

To limit another human being from obeying the will of God for one's life is to cheat that individual out of something good from God. To limit anyone from carrying out their God-given assignment is to rob future generations from advancement.

Can you imagine Bill Gates being arrested for giving us Microsoft? Can you imagine the Wright brothers going to prison for giving us the airplane? Can you imagine Thomas Edison being hung from a tree by his neck for giving us the lightbulb? What a great contribution these men made to society! My point is this: it would be a shame to kill a dreamer, no matter what gender or race they happen to be.

When the fire of a dream burns inside, you become willing to die for it. I've always felt that if I didn't somehow get this book out of me, my purpose for living would not be fully accomplished. Our call, as women, is just that strong.

As a people, somewhere deep down in our souls, God engraved truth in us Blacks, and in time we stood for what we believed—even though many died for the cause. How can anyone be so cruel as to deny another human being his God-given gift and to exalt his own thinking above the thoughts of God for the life and future of another, as the slave master did to my ancestors in days gone by? It took us a long time to recover from such cruelty. Some of my people are still learning to forgive, because their hurt went so deep. Thank God for Jesus going to the cross and setting us free, free to forgive and never inflict that kind of pain on anyone else.

I also thank God for people like Fredrick Douglas, Booker T. Washington, Sojourner Truth and Harriet Tubman, just to name a few, who fought for African-American rights. Every woman who has been discriminated against in ministry can understand that struggle. And just as we had to win our battle for civil rights, we women must now win our ecclesiastical rights.

Hey, God, I'm a Woman; Can You Use Me?!

CHAPTER 8

THE DAY I ANSWERED THE CALL

Let no man despise thy youth; but be thou an example of the believers, in word, in conversation, in charity, in spirit, in faith, in purity. Till I come, give attendance to reading, to exhortation, to doctrine. Neglect not the gift that is in thee, which was given thee by prophecy, with the laying on of the hands of the presbytery.

Meditate upon these things; give thyself wholly to them; that thy profiting may appear to all. Take heed unto thyself, and unto the doctrine; continue in them: for in doing this thou shalt both save thyself, and them that hear thee. 1 Timothy 4:12-16

Before we get to more about the Gnostics, let me share with you a little of my own testimony, how I answered the call of God. I have always been in love with God and somehow knew in my heart, even as a young child, that I would walk and talk with Him one day. It wasn't until 1979 that I started to cry out to Him, "God, if it's possible to have a real relationship with You, I want it," but I didn't know how to began such a relationship.

I remembered seeing older people talking with God. When they had problems, they would go to what they called their "prayer closet," and, not long afterward, they would come out with the answer they needed. I would hear them talking among themselves, saying "I had a little talk with Jesus, and He made it all right" In my mind, that was power, and I wanted it. Today, many years later, I can say that Christ is my power Source!

I was blessed to have a mother of great faith. She raised ten children on her own, and there were times when she would gather us all together and have us pray. She instilled in us the fact that God was real and that He cared for us enough to make a way in difficult times. I watched her struggle to keep food on the table and clothes on our backs. She worked hard to give us the best education she possibly could. I know she did it with the grace of God. Mother also kept us in private schools.

At the age of fifteen, I decided to run away from home, and for nearly two years, Mother didn't know if I was alive or dead. She never gave up her search for me, and eventually found me, with the help of the police. I was reunited with my family, but not long afterward, I left Mississippi and moved to California.

In Los Angeles, I began dating a guy who introduced me to the drug known as PCP. Until then, I had never put anything stronger than marijuana into my body. We went out that night to a house party, and someone pulled out the drugs while we were playing cards. At one point, the host began to pass around a very funny-smelling cigarette, and when it came my turn, I said, "No, thank you."

My boyfriend said, "Try it! You'll like it! It's just like marijuana." So I took some.

Very quickly I started to feel like a midget. I felt like I was too small to even get the card up on the table where we were sitting in the dining room. So that I would not embarrass myself, I asked if I could use the restroom because the drug was too strong for my system.

Once inside the bathroom, I felt faint, so I came out and asked if I could lie down on the couch. The host said, "Sure!" and asked if I was okay. The rest continued to play cards.

When I laid down, I quickly descended into outer darkness. By that, I mean that I began going down into a hole, or pit, and the blackness of it was indescribable. Even to this day, I have difficulty expressing what it was like. I knew I had left earth, and there was no way back. Fear gripped me, and I could see my mother on her knees, praying. I cried out, "Jesus, help me!"

All of a sudden, two presences walked up to that pit I had been descending into. I knew instantly who they were. Jesus was on the right side, and Satan was on the left. I never actually saw either one of them, but I didn't have to see them with my natural eye to know what was happening. There was a fight on for my soul. In the Spirit realm you don't have to see to know.

I heard swords clanking, and within a matter of seconds, Jesus commissioned me to go back to earth and preach the Gospel. I said, "Lord, I will." Immediately I was back in my body, and the high was over. I sat up on that couch and knew that I had to get out of that place.

We had been raised Catholic, but my sister was attending a Bible-believing church and had invited me to go with her several times, to no avail. That night, however, I knew that I must go to church with her. No one had to convince me that God was real. I had experienced Him firsthand.

I went on a Tuesday night. After the preacher finished teaching that night, he gave an altar call. I wanted to go down so badly, but I didn't want all those people looking at me. There were more than a thousand people there at that Tuesday night Bible study.

The preacher said, "If you would like to receive Jesus Christ as your personal Lord and Savior, come down here."

Oh, how I wanted to go, but something said to me (in my mind), "Don't you go down there and get embarrassed!" So I remained in my seat.

Then, all of a sudden, my knees started to shake, and I couldn't control them. I heard the preacher say, "I don't do this often, but there's a person here, and the Lord is calling you. You need to come down here. In fact, your knees are shaking right now."

I thought to myself, "How could he know?" I was sitting toward the back of that great crowd. Shaken, I asked Jesus to come into my heart there where I was sitting, and the physical shaking stopped.

In the days to come, I just could not stop going to that church, but because I didn't know my way around the area yet, I always went with my sister. One Tuesday night, I got off work and was looking forward to the Bible study. When I got to my sister's house, she said, "We're not going to the Bible study tonight."

I thought to myself, "Oh no! Then I'll have to go alone." My brother-in-law gave me directions, but I got lost, and was wondering how I would ever find my way to the church in the dark (we didn't have cell phones in those days) when I spotted an LAPD cruiser passing me. I got an idea. I sped up, flashed my high beam lights at him and pulled him over. When he came to my car window, he wasn't very happy.

"What's the matter?" he asked.

"Officer, could you help me," I pleaded. "I'm lost, and I'm trying to find a big church. They're having this incredible Bible study."

He told me how to get to the church, but before he got back in his cruiser, he said, "Young lady, don't you ever flag down a policeman like that again." I apologized, explaining that I was from a small town in the South and didn't know you couldn't stop a policeman that way. In the South that would not have been a problem.

I went to that church for three months before I got up the courage to go down to the front and acknowledge that I had given my life to Jesus. It had been January of 1980 when I went with my sister for the first time, and it was now March 25. When I went to the front, I was filled with the Holy Spirit, with the evidence of speaking in my heavenly prayer language.

When Jesus told me to go and preach His Word, I'd had no idea that there was any controversy about women in ministry. But I was in for a rude awakening! Before long, I started hearing things like, "Women are not supposed to teach or preach. They should never usurp authority over a man."

I thought, "What is this?" For me, it was totally confusing, because I knew what Jesus had told me to do. I was a new Christian, but I had enough sense to know that God would never go against His own Word. I began to make the confusing statements I was hearing a matter of prayer. The Lord encouraged me to study, and I was so thankful for the precious

Holy Spirit, my Teacher. It was not long after that when God birthed in my spirit the title of this book: *Hey God, I'm A Woman; Can You Use Me?*

I carried this growing baby for many years, until God sent a lovely prophet by the name of Andre Asby to tell me that it was now time to release the message. It felt like I was giving birth, and a load actually lifted from me. I've already said it once, but I must say it again. I love and honor God, and if He had said in His Word that a woman speaking publicly was against His will, I would be the first to sit down. That's not what He said, and it's time that we all recognize it.

Hey, God, I'm a Woman; Can You Use Me?!

CHAPTER 9

THE CULTURAL SITUATION BEHIND PAUL'S WORDS

But I suffer not a woman to teach nor usurp authority over the man but to be in silence. For Adam was first formed then Eve. 1 Timothy 2:12-13

Now that we have this background, let's get back to one of the specific texts that have caused confusion in this question of the proper role of women in the Church today. Did Paul mean this particular passage to apply to every woman everywhere? That's a question worth examining. As we have noted, too many times we believe and repeat things that we've never actually checked out.

There are several things to be considered here. For one, the translation of Hebrew and Greek into English has always been a very complex matter. For another, do we ever stop to consider the culture and times in which the Bible was written? Should we ask if Paul perhaps had a motive for making such a statement? Or should we just read our Bibles and say, "Forget it, regardless of who gets hurt." If you have read this far, or if you just skipped over other sections and got here, please hear me out now, and then go do some honest research of your own on this matter.

Again, Paul is writing a letter to his spiritual son Timothy to encourage him in the city of Ephesus. Ephesus was an interesting city. The people were into goddess worship, and their temple to the goddess Diana was so magnificent that it was considered to be one of the seven wonders of the ancient world.

The gods of Ephesus were all female, and the men who participated in the temple worship were all ceremonially castrated. The goddess worshippers were not modest in their dress and behavior, for the goddesses themselves were not modest. The mountain fertility goddess, known as Kybele, was often depicted as being topless.

Goddess worship in Ephesus was loud, boisterous and sexually immoral. Lying with temple prostitutes was seen as a way for the men of Ephesus to experience the divine nature. This was the climate of the day in which Paul's letter to Timothy was written.

So Timothy had a serious situation on his hand, and Paul had to write to him and address certain issues that were slowly creeping into the church. Christianity was a young religion, and woman needed to know at the outset that Christian women did not conduct themselves in this manner. If they had done so before knowing Christ, that was understandable, but after becoming a Christian, they were expected to live a different kind of life.

I believe, therefore, that the instructions given by Paul to Timothy were for a specific people (those in the church at Ephesus) at a specific time (the first century) in a specific place Asia Minor, and it was because goddess worship and matriarchal dominance were so prevalent there.

There is another reason. The religious sect of that day called the Gnostic, the group we mentioned in an earlier chapter, believed that Eve was the mother of all living, including Adam, and this and other false doctrines were creeping into the church. Paul had a responsibility to encourage Timothy not to let that false doctrine in, so he told him clearly:

> *For Adam was first formed then Eve.*
>
> 1 Timothy 2:13

While Paul *does* appear to restrict women from speaking in two specific places in the Scriptures, he did this because of the social environment of that day. He was not making a rule for all time.

This again reminds me of what slaves had to endure here in America and elsewhere. There were those who could take the teachings of the Bible and apparently prove that slavery was the will of God. At the same time, there were those who could take the same Bible and prove that slavery was not God's best for humanity. Paul was advising people how to live in the first century in pagan Ephesus, not writing a rule for all generations to come.

Women have always been active in the service of the Lord, even though they were often considered to be second-class citizens. At Pentecost, Peter confirmed this:

> *But this is that which was spoken by the prophet Joel; and it shall come to pass in the last days, saith God, I will pour out of my Spirit upon all flesh: and your sons and your DAUGHTERS shall prophesy, and your young men shall see visions, and your old men shall dream dreams: and on my servants and on my HANDMAIDENS I will pour out in those days of my Spirit; and they shall prophesy.* Acts 2:16-18 (Emphasis mine)

Later, Philip, known as *"the evangelist,"* had four daughters who prophesied (see Acts 21:9). How could they do that if women everywhere were never to speak and especially to men?

Paul was not at all opposed to women in ministry. If we do our studies, keeping it all in context, we will have a correct understanding of why Paul had to bring correction in the first-century churches. For instance, Acts 17 and 18 give us insight into the corruption that was going on in Paul's day. But Acts 17 also mentions *"honourable women"* (Acts 17:12). He mentioned one of them by name—Damaris (Verse 34). This woman must have been important to Paul (and the Holy Spirit). She was said to have been among a group who *"clave unto him [Paul], and believed."* In other words, she accepted and supported the Gospel.

Paul had other women assisting him in ministry. He was clearly not against women (just as Jesus had not been). In Acts 18, we read about a man named Aquila, but we also read about his wife Priscilla (see verse 2). Later we see this pair together expounding, or teaching, Apollos on the deeper truths in God (verse 26). Yes, Priscilla taught, and she taught men.

So women were accepted by Paul to function in public ministry, in spite of what the church today tries to do to shut us down through their lack of knowledge.

A woman named Junia (see Romans 16:7) was even known as an apostle. Later, the translators, no doubt because of prejudice, apparently adjusted the female name Junia into the male name Junias (which name did not exist in ancient times).

Was Paul confused? He also wrote the letter to the Galatians, in which he said:

> *There is neither Jew or Greek, there is neither bond nor free, there is neither male nor female: for you are all one in Christ Jesus.* Galatians 3:28

This is the general, universal principle that we all live by. So what is our conclusion? It was the cultural situation in Ephesus that sparked Paul to write Timothy what he did. It was nothing against women or against women in ministry and should never be applied in that way.

Hey, God, I'm a Woman; Can You Use Me?!

CHAPTER 10

WHAT, THEN?

Let your woman keep silent in the churches; for it is not permitted unto them to speak; but they are commanded to be under obedience, as also saith the law. And if they will learn any thing let them ask their husbands at home; for it is a shame for women to speak in the church.

1 Corinthians 14:34-35

The question remains, Why, then, did Paul forbid women from speaking in the Church. And was he forbidding women to speak at all, even to pray or prophesy in public? Most importantly, was he forbidding women from participating in public ministry?

The main verse that constitutes the foundation of all that Paul says is 1 Corinthians 14:33. It states:

For God is not the author of confusion but of peace, as in all the churches of the saints.

1 Corinthians 14:33

The instruction of Paul is found in verse 39:

> *Therefore, my brethren desire earnestly to prophesy.* 1 Corinthians 14:39

By this, Paul meant that we should be zealous about giving forth the Word of God, for prophecy was the main way of preaching in the first century. In verse 40, Paul states:

> *But let all things be done decently and in order.*
> 1 Corinthians 14:40

This is a principle that applies to all churches.

How does this apply to women? It's very simple.

Women were not yet able to attend school in that day, so they usually did not attend public lectures of any kind. Then along came Christianity, with its liberty for women, and, for the first time, they were allowed to have this privilege. In their excitement over this turn of events, they would interrupt the services, asking their husbands, "Honey, what does that mean?" So Paul was instructing them to ask questions of their husband (who had an education and could explain things to them) at home. In this way, Paul was dealing with order, nothing more.

This teaching does not have any other application, and to use it to forbid women to participate in ministry in the twenty-first century is a gross miscarriage of justice that grieves the heart of God and hinders the progress of the Church of Jesus Christ.

I have a deep conviction that the present treatment of women in a large segment of the Body of Christ does *not* reflect the mind of Christ. The woman at the well was proof of that. When she left home that day she didn't know she had an appointment with Jesus, just as I didn't know that I had an appointment with Him that fateful night in California. He just shows up when we least expect it, and He changes our lives forever—no matter what gender we happen to be.

And if God has called and commissioned us to carry out an assignment in His name, then we'd better obey Him. If Jesus tarries, there will be a new generation coming up beneath us that will need a springboard from which to launch. They can take up where we have left off. So you and I are responsible for that next generation, and we must leave a legacy for them to continue.

In this book, we've been asking, *"Hey, God, I'm a Woman; Can You Use Me?!"* but God's not at all confused on this issue, and He never has been. He knows the high purpose for which He has created women. We're the ones who are confused. I pray that some of that confusion is now lifting and that together—men and women of God—we can march forward into our glorious destiny.

Ministry Page

You may contact the author at the following address:

FRUIT OF THE SPIRIT MINISTRIES
1100 Hickox Street
Santa Fe, NM 87505

505-660-5282